The Field Guide to Telecommuting: The Definitive Handbook for Current and Potential Teleworkers

Catherine Rayburn-Trobaugh

The Field Guide to Telecommuting: The Definitive Handbook for Current and Potential Teleworkers

By Catherine Rayburn-Trobaugh

Word Branch Publishing
Marble, NC
2012

Catherine Rayburn-Trobaugh

Published by Word Branch Publishing

No part of this document may be reproduced or transmitted in any form or by any means, electronic, mechanical, photocopying, recording, or otherwise, without prior written permission of Word Branch Publishing.

PO Box 474
Marble, NC 28905

http://wordbranch.com

Library of Congress Control Number: 2013930131
ISBN-13:978-0615680958
ISBN-10:061568095X

Table of Contents

The Field Guide to Telecommuting

Dedication

To my dad, Winfield Rayburn, for being courageous and adventurous and being my inspiration in so many ways.

I'd also like to thank my dear friend and partner, my husband Bill, for his patience and support, and my daughters, Vicki and Amanda for making me laugh.

And a big thanks goes to my telecommuting contributors Gayle Brown, Esther Driggs and Lisa Godfrey , to Don Dingee for graciously writing the foreword and to Matt Savage for his insight into management.

The Field Guide to Telecommuting

Foreword

In the near past, many people went to work in factories and made something. In a linear process of designing, building, selling, and supporting products, employees clocked in at 7:59, worked until lunch break, returned for more work and clocked out at 5:01.

The present is all new. Technology changes jobs and makes information available via networks. Complex products are built almost anywhere, cheaply, and shipped anywhere. Families often are dual-income or women-led households. Mobile devices make instant connections a reality.

Telecommuting is the new "where" of work for many people, and it's more than taking work home – it's being engaged in collaboration. People located anywhere interact in a continuous, non-linear dance of information, products and services, ideas and lifestyles.

Employees (and freelancers) still develop and sell products and services but now are distributed across states and countries in a flatter structure with less oversight and more collaboration on multiple projects. Customers have a voice in design and assembly of customized offerings and expect real-time service with consistency and frequent delight. Prospects have more information and fewer preconceived notions, sifting through social networks and online media and search tools, talking with employees and customers for insight before buying.

Whether you are in a home office, a facility, a library, a park or a Starbucks with online access, you can collaborate in this exciting new dance. You can jump in at any time and instantly see what's happening, who is talking about it, and help the next thing happen by sharing your ideas.

Catherine's guide helps those considering the leap into telecommuting, from the occasional out-of-office day, to the full-time business that tests concentration, perseverance and self-marketing skills. First time telecommuters will find things they may not have considered in a chapter on getting started, and there is a chapter with advice from seasoned pros.

For the experienced telecommuter, Catherine looks at ideas of how to find work, and how not to find it. There are pointers on how to set up an office, organize activity, and get and stay motivated. She also has thoughtful chapters on some of the resistance you might encounter and on when it might be time to make adjustments, or change direction entirely.

As a fellow "dog dodger," I'm happy recommending Catherine's thoughts and experience in telecommuting as an aid to all of us adapting to this new where of work.

Don Dingee writes and speaks on social computing at http://L2MyOwnDevices.com

Preface

As a second generation telecommuter, it felt natural for me to step into the role. My father had worked side jobs as an engineer decades before the word telecommuting was in existence. It was merely called moonlighting, and this seemed to give it a sinister edge. In the 21st century, telecommuting has become an accepted step in the technological progression, and, at least for some industries, works as well, if not better, than traditional commuting.

After years of part-time teaching at the college level and taking my work home with me, I was familiar with the concept. I rarely had an office at the schools where I worked, and it was easier for me to do class planning and grading early in the morning before I went to my "day job" of marketing. I always felt more productive and in control working from home, and I enjoyed my breaks more in my own kitchen than in a dreary company lunchroom.

When my husband retired after 27 years in law enforcement, we decided to move to an area that we had always loved in Western North Carolina and immediately fell in love with a remote creek-side mountain home nestled up against a national forest. The only way to get to the house was a one-lane gravel road with a mountain on one side and a 300 foot drop on the other—impassable in bad weather. Coupled with the fact that the main industry in the county was tourism and outdoor adventures, I knew I had to make working at home full time a reality.

I was lucky enough to be offered a writing class to teach at a nearby community college, and a few months later, through a relative's connection, I got my first work-at-home job with Wiley-Blackwell Publishing as a marketing representative. Since this still came to less than 25 hours a week, I had to be inventive to come up with more. Little by little, I stitched together a full-time, freelance telecommuting career.

Over the years, I've had a number of fulfilling and even fun jobs. I've gotten to do a little traveling, spend time with my family and work in comfort in a familiar office even though I change jobs frequently.

Conventional workers are naturally curious, and sometimes envious, about telecommuting. Most people at one time or another have fantasized about working from home. After answering numerous questions about how I got started and how they could work from home, I realized I had something to offer to potential and current teleworkers, and I came up with the concept of *The Field Guide to Telecommuting.*

On the surface, telecommuting seems like the ideal job situation—and for many it is. Telecommuting often offers flexible hours and the commute is pretty easy. It's a greener lifestyle and saves cash on transportation. And as many telecommuters point out, you can work in your jammies if you choose. But on the downside, it requires commitment to put the necessary time in and not get distracted by the usual household disturbances. It may involve intensive self-marketing and most often gaps in income if you are a freelancer. You will have to contend with neighbors and relatives, not to mention the occasional manager, who don't see it as "real work." One of the goal's I had in writing this book is to present a realistic look at telecommuting to help people decide whether or not it is for them.

I call this book a field guide for several reasons. I'm an avid outdoor's person, and field guides play a big role in my personal life. I like the way they are laid out: easy to find information quickly, and if I don't need a section, I don't have to muddle through it to find what I want. On the other hand, I've often read field guides cover to cover to get an overview of the subject. They are rough, tough no-nonsense books that have the versatility to be both entertaining and sources of valuable information.

The Field Guide to Telecommuting is a book for potential, new and seasoned telecommuters. I've gathered data and tips from numerous sources including other telecommuters, employment agencies, human resource professionals, government sources and my own experience. It's laid out in an easy-to-read format that can be read from cover to cover or in sections. Included between headings are highlights of companies, organizations and helpful facts that I've "sighted" throughout my research journey. I've included information that would be valuable to freelancers, consultants and those who telework for a single company. Choose what you need from this book, and save the rest for when and if you need it.

At the end of this guide is a resource page that contains links to helpful sites for telecommuters. I researched all of the links when I put the list together, but be wise. Sites can change over time and may not be as useful or as straightforward as they once were so be judicious. In addition to the list in the book, I put together a web page strictly for people who have purchased this guide:http://wordbranch.com/the-field-guide-to-telecommuting-resource-page.html. You'll also find an office equipment shopping list, a PDF version of this guide and other handy items. I will update it as needed, and I welcome all suggestions. You can also sign up for a monthly newsletter about telecommuting on the site to stay current with trends and issues.

I hope you find *The Field Guide to Telecommuting* useful and easy to use. If you have any suggestions or questions, please feel free to email me at catherine@wordbranch.com.

Catherine Rayburn-Trobaugh

Chapter 1: Telecommuting Defined

Simply defined, telecommuting is the ability to work away from a physical workplace using technology to take the place of a traditional on-site office. In reality, telecommuting, or telework, encompasses much more. Telecommuters might be freelancers, work full-time or part-time for a company or agency, work at home only occasionally, all the time or part of the time. They may work at home, an independent office or at a remote office set up by their organization. It encompasses a wide range of industries, job descriptions and pay rates.

The history of telecommuting reaches back decades. The term telecommuting was coined in the late 70s when advancements in telecommunications made it more realistic for some industries to provide at least part time telecommuting options to employees. The state of California developed the first large scale program in 1987 in order to bring down costs and pollution caused by the massive commuting of government workers. By 2002, the program had grown from 200 during the pilot state to more than 2,000. The program continues today with a possible expansion in the future to help save more money for the state government. i

While the Bureau of Labor defines telework as working from home or out of the office at least once a month, individuals have varying opinions as to what consists of telecommuting. One person's view of reasonable telework might be an occasional Friday working at home, and others telecommute full time. An estimated 40 percent of the telecommuting labor force works 20 to 30 hours a week from home or other off-site locations, but work at home options include a large variety of choices depending on industry and employer.

Who Is Telecommuting?

With 2.8 million Americans telecommuting to some extent, and more joining the ranks every year, it is clear that this is a trend that is rising. Although the numbers wavered somewhat though the recession, the percentage of telecommuters are expected to rise with the general employment rate. As our perception of careers and the workplace continue to evolve, the idea of telework will become more acceptable as an alternative to traditional working conditions.

Some industries are a natural for telecommuting. Artists, musicians and writers have been working from home since long before most industries considered it an option. As technology increased, so did the viability to work somewhere other than a traditional office. As early as the 70s, computer programmers and other tech specialists saw an opportunity to get out of the office. With the use of the Internet it became possible for more technology minded teleworkers to stay out of the office more and more.

With the development of the World Wide Web in 1992, and the introduction of faster and cheaper computers into the marketplace, the face of telecommuting changed rapidly. A new realm of possibilities opened for non-techies to jump into the teleworkforce. And they did. By 2001 there were more than 15 million teleworkers. Currently, most industries can support telecommuting at least on a part-time level.

The demographics of the telecommuting workforce may be surprising. Most are males between the ages of 45 and 54, and over 50 percent have a household income of more than $75,000. More than half of federal employees can telecommute through the federal Telework program, and 50 million workers have the possibility of working from home.

The locations of teleworking are surprising as well. While more than 60 percent of telecommuting work from home, 40 percent of those interviewed did some work in their cars while others chose to work in parks, coffee shops and libraries.ii

> **Sighted: The Telecommute News**
> *The Telecommute News shares a wealth of information for anyone who is telecommuting or wants to telecommute. In addition to current articles about telework, they have a website review section, job notices and tons of resources.*
> *http://www.telecommutenews.com*

With the incredible diversity of jobs, workers and workplaces, it's no surprise that it is predicted that teleworking will become more common that traditional work sites in years to come.

To Be or Not to Be a Teleworker

While telecommuting seems like the ideal work situation to many people, there are a number of things to consider before making the plunge.

- Is telecommuting appropriate for your job and industry? Not all industries, or jobs within the industry, will sustain telecommuting. Talk it over carefully with your supervisor and human resource people before you decide to make it a reality. Some workplaces are just resistant to teleworking for reasons discussed elsewhere in this book.
- Do you have a home office space that can accommodate your work-at-home needs? Look around your on-site office and imagine it in your home. While there are amazing organizational and space-saving tools, consider the space you need for any given project.
- Is your workspace quiet and conducive to concentration and good work habits? While some people can work with a hurricane going on around them, many can't. If you need to be on the phone, you'll

need to quiet the background noises even if you can concentrate through them.

- If you are a self-employed home worker, do you have the funds to cover dry spells? And there WILL be dry spells. You'll need to develop good saving habits to keep back money for taxes, insurance and the inevitable emergencies, not to mention unpaid sick days, that will arise.
- Do you have the capital to begin your stay-at-home business? Sometimes it is as inexpensive as a laptop and a telephone, but most of the time it isn't. Consider the cost of possible travel, supplies, inventory (if applicable), the cost of hiring professionals like attorneys, accountants etc.
- How does your family feel about telecommuting? Many people erroneously see telework as not "real" work. If a spouse has this conception, and you can't change it, it may cause real friction. Kids are often the most resistant. If mommy/daddy is at home, it must mean that she/he isn't working.

Telecommuting has obvious real advantages to consider. Some typical work costs will decrease:

sweats cost a lot less than suits; gas, wear and tear on a vehicle and commuting costs are minimized, and lunches out at restaurants will turn into lunches in the kitchen. And the commute itself is easy— mine consists of dodging the dogs in the hallway to make my way to my office. I can deal with that kind of traffic jam. Since I live next to a national forest, instead of coffee breaks in the lunchroom, I can take a walk in the woods.

So with all of this idyllic work time, what's the down side? Some of the pluses are minuses too. A walk in the woods can turn into a way to avoid work; wearing sweats all the time can turn you into a real slob, and eating another hastily made cheese sandwich can make you long for the days of servers and menus. There are days it takes real self-discipline to finish unsavory projects and even more days when household interruptions make working nearly impossible.

If you are lucky enough to work for a company or organization that has a telecommuting plan or is willing to consider one, then you may also be lucky enough to be able to test the waters without risking much. Try a few days a week or month to start with and build from there if it suits you, but if it doesn't, don't be reluctant to admit it. Some people are better suited for telework than others just like some people like chocolate and others vanilla—it's just a matter of preference.

On the other hand, don't give up too easily. Just like any other work situation, there good days and bad, and there's a pretty steep learning curve to find your natural rhythm and to create your own schedule that works for you. Give it time.

If you are venturing out on your own, consider a few things before you turn in your notice. How are your finances? As with a physical business, it is doubtful that you'll start out turning a profit right away whatever

Sighted: The US Government

The federal government has become one of the largest and most active proponents of telecommuting in the US. The Telework Enhancement Act of 2010 makes it possible for more than 10,000 federal employees to telecommute at least on a part-time basis. In the 2010 report to congress, the teleworkers' program reported that job satisfaction and retention levels were higher than non-teleworkers. The plan has been so successful that future plans include increasing supervisors' telecommuting which has lagged behind.

industry you may be in. If you have outstanding loans and credit cards, pay them off before you make the plunge. Remember that health and life insurance will have to be paid out of pocket, and these expenses can be considerable. If you aren't capable of being relatively debt-free and don't have a nest egg put away, then telecommuting may not be for you.

Find people in your own industry that work at home and see what they think. Social networks are a good place to start. LinkedIn caters to professionals in general, and your job description may have its own network. Ask around and you'll probably find a few people who are willing to share their experiences.

Mentally picture yourself through the work week. What can you easily do at home? Are there technologies and computer programs that can help you overcome the barriers? Do a little legwork to find out what is available.

If you just know you want or need to telecommute without a particular skill set, do a little digging into realistic possibilities. More service industry jobs are being offered as work-at-home opportunities, but beware. There are a lot of scams mixed in with the legitimate offerings. Read the chapter on scams before you commit to a job, and NEVER pay to work.

If you are in good financial condition and you have a good plan, telework can be rewarding and freeing. You will be saving money, helping the environment, having at least partial control of your schedule and finding a new level of productivity and job satisfaction.

The Green Worker

One of my passions in life is the protecting the environment. I was raised to have a respect for the ecology of our planet, and since moving to a delicate ecosystem, this commitment has become even stronger. I've worked hard to create an office with a minimal carbon footprint including using recycled paper products, conducting nearly all business virtually and using a webhost that is entirely run by wind energy. Telecommuting not only fits my needs as a worker but also my commitment as a conservationist.

The statistics for even half-time telecommuting and energy savings are impressive. If all workers who have potential telecommuting jobs were to work half of their hours at home, the dependence on foreign oil would decrease by nearly 50 percent while reducing carbon emissions by half. This is not taking into consideration hidden costs that are more difficult to estimate like roadway costs, construction and office equipment. Avoiding traffic jams can save a quarter of a million tons of greenhouse gases annually.

If the ecological savings aren't important to you, how about this: telecommuting decreases the possibility of both pandemics and terrorist attacks by reducing the amount of time people spend in large groups. Telework can bring jobs back to the US from foreign markets and boost the national productivity up to 55 percent as well as significantly reducing auto accidents. iii

Any way that you look at it, telecommuting can contribute to a cleaner and safer lifestyle. State and federal governments are becoming more aware of the energy, thus money savings, and creating plans to encourage telework. Companies are getting on board to reduce operating costs and to be responsible stewards. From oil savings and reducing wear on automobiles to diminishing the effects of global warming, telecommuting is clearly the greener way to work.

Chapter 2: Getting Started

If you've decided that telecommuting is for you, then you have a few more decisions to make. If you're fortunate, it's as simple as telling your employer that you want to take part in an already established program. But for most people it takes a little more time and work.

 If you are currently at a job where telecommuting is a possibility but not a given, and you want to stay with that organization, and then trace down the person or office you need to contact. Read your employee handbook to see if there is a program already in place and ask the human resource administrator about options. Often the first stop should be your immediate supervisor; after all, he or she has to be on board with the concept. Some supervisors are suspicious of the whole work-at-home idea believing that if workers are not directly supervised at all times than they must be goofing off. But others are open to the possibility and may have had personal experience with it.

You may have to prove to your boss that telecommuting is not just a legitimate option for millions of workers but that productivity is not only equal to on-site workers but nearly always exceeds expectations. Not only does the US federal government have a work-at-home program, but some of the largest most successful corporations in the world have found it a successful alternative. The resource section of this book will give you fodder for your argument.

Another possibility that may help sway a reluctant boss is to work with him or her to develop a part-time, trial telecommute. Start out working from home one day a week or even an afternoon or morning to begin. Develop a plan with your supervisor to set goals and measure productivity, and set a review date no sooner than six weeks after you begin telecommuting. Of course this means you'll have to work hard to make the grade—perhaps even harder than you do on-site, but it's worth it in the end. After you prove that you can be successful at telecommuting, then ask for an increase in off-site time until you have a balance that you and your manager are comfortable with.

Under all circumstances, you will also need to check in with your company's human resource department. HR can let you know if there is a program in place that your supervisor may not have know about or if there are other precedents that help or hurt your case and whether or not there are policies in motion related to teleworking. They should be familiar, at least in theory, with the concept and up-to-date with the latest developments and news.

Types of Jobs

Some types of jobs lend themselves better to telecommuting than others. Writers and artists are among the original teleworkers, but technology has opened the doors for many more professions to join the ranks. Think creatively and be aware of technology that can help you successfully work from home, and don't forget that you have the option to freelance or consult as well as work for an organization. The lists below are by no means comprehensive, but they can help guide you into possibilities given your own talents and interests.

Freelance Jobs:

- Writer
- Artist
- Graphic artist
- Programmer
- Editing
- Design
- Virtual concierge
- Craft person
- Accountant

Positions with Companies:

- Telemarketing
- Virtual assistant
- Transcription
- Data entry
- Customer service
- Tutor
- Human resource professional
- Translator
- Mock juror
- Virtual Help Desk

Sighted: Deloitte
This accounting firm was named Best Company for Telecommuting in 2011 by CNN Money. Known for its diverse workforce and out of the box thinking, 86% of Deloitte's employees are regular telecommuters.

On Deloitte's "Careers" webpage, they highlight some of their employees who have interesting hobbies and side careers like an Olympic contender, a part time rock star and a mountain climber. Deloitte prides itself on focusing on their talent and this has landed them consistently on Fortune Magazine's Top 100 Companies to Work For.

These lists could go on for pages, and many of the positions can be done either as a consultant or employee. The versatility of teleworking stretches as far as your imagination can take it.

Defining Talents, Education and Experience

We all have an image of what we ideally would like to be doing for a living—sometimes this is realistic and sometimes not. If you have a passion for writing but you don't have any experience or education in that direction, then you may want to build the qualifications to be successful before you quit your day job. Conversely, you may have a Master's in accounting and a decade of experience, but if you don't feel that this is the field you want to continue to work in then a reassessment may be in order.

So what are the first steps in finding your dream telecommuting job if your present workplace doesn't offer the option? The US Department of Labor provides links to career assessment tools that can be helpful if you truly don't know what direction to go. O*Net is a national depository of labor data and it also offers interest and ability profile tools. They can be a little complicated, but stick with it--it can be very valuable. I've provided the link in the reference section.

It's always helpful to do an honest evaluation of your skills, talents and education before you jump into to a real commitment. And honesty is key. You aren't stretching the facts on your resume; you are kidding yourself and that can cost both money and time. At the same time, don't sell yourself short. Consider all of the non-paying as well as paid positions you've held, different types of training and hobbies and talents you have that you may not have considered as money makers. Sit down and make some lists to focus your thoughts. The following can help you organize your thoughts and create a pro/con inventory of what you have to offer.

Education: In addition to formal education, what other types of training do you have regardless of field?

- College and graduate school
- Trade school
- Apprenticeships
- Certifications
- Online training
- On-the-job training
- Self taught

Skills: What do you excel at—right now?

- Professional
- Hobbies
- Volunteer work
- Interests

Experience: Even consider jobs that you had a number of years ago as well as recent.

- Current jobs
- Past jobs
- Volunteer jobs
- Military
- Part time
- Self employment

> ### *Sighted: Telework Tools*
> *Telework Tools is a research organization funded primarily by government agencies. Although its primary function is to provide information to workers with disabilities, the tools and information are helpful to anyone who is interested in telecommuting. Included in the available information is an assessment test, lists of possible professions and links to other agencies that promote telework.*
>
> *http://www.teleworktools.org/*

Career Interests: Dream a little here as well as being realistic.

- The dream job
- A modified version of the dream job
- A career that you envied
- Something you think you'd be good at, but haven't tried
- A previous job
- A present job

Needs: After all that dreaming, it's time to come back to earth. What do you need for you and your family out of a telecommuting job?

- The minimum amount of money
- The ideal amount of money
- Hours
- Days of the week
- Promotions

After making a list of your interests and pros and cons, do some reality checks. One of the biggest issues might be whether or not you have the ability to work on your own and concentrate at home. If you've never been good at self-motivation, then you probably won't get better by telecommuting. Granted, the longer you work on your own, the better you get at time management, but some people just aren't comfortable with it.

Additionally, how your spouse or partner feels about it will make an enormous difference as to your success or failure. Someone who supports you will make the lean times bearable, but if your partner doesn't see telecommuting as "real work," then chances are you won't feel like it has value. Have an honest talk with him or her focusing on both the perks and the disadvantages and follow through from there.

Websites and Social Networking

It is virtually, pun intended, impossible to telecommute in the 21st century without the World Wide Web, and who would want to? The Internet makes it realistic for nearly everyone to set up shop quickly and inexpensively with seemingly limitless options. That, of course, is the downside too. Because anyone can do it, everyone is doing it—or so it seems. Your challenge is to stand out from the crowd.

Once again, the key to successful and efficient use of the Internet is a careful assessment. Before you jump into the overwhelming world of social networking or spend money and time on a website, decide what your personal and family needs are, what your job/industry needs are, who you are trying to reach and why. Certainly freelancers and consultants use Internet options more to attract and keep business, but the wage earner can benefit too.

Far too many employees, both traditional and teleworkers, have found out the hard way that the Internet can be an unforgiving place too. Remember at all times that your professional persona is on trial and very public. Use the same common sense that you would if you were at a physical workplace talking to other employees—keep it professional.

If are teleworking for an organization, social networks can help keep you in touch with your colleagues and peers. LinkedIn is a particularly good professional network, but check to see if your industry has one unique to your field. Your organization may have a network specifically for employees or clients. SalesForce is one of the nation's largest networks and is custom fit for each organization. If your association doesn't have a way for telecommuters and in-house employees to connect, you may consider starting a network. It can go a long way to beat the isolation that sometimes comes with telecommuting.

Freelancers and Consultants

Freelancers work entirely on their own and are responsible for their own marketing, work schedule and contacts. Freelancing gives the telecommuter the most flexibility, but it's probably the most work too, and the hours can get crazy at times. Freelancers should take full advantage of the Web—it is merely an extension of the home office, and it should feel that way.

A consultant is similar and works in much the same way as a freelancer. However, a consultant is usually hired for his or her expertise and advises organizations in the given field. Instead of offering a product related service, like writing or programming, a consultant offers the benefit of expert guidance.

For freelancers and consultants, social networking is a valuable tool but beware of getting caught up in networking for networking's sake. I've heard successful telecommuters say that social networking is worthless and others that can't stop singing the praises. I fall somewhere in the middle. I focus on one—Facebook—and I use a social media management system to send messages to other. I have found some success through social media as free advertisement, so it is certainly worth the effort.

If you intend on freelancing, you should first connect with others in your field, and one of the best place to do that is through social networking. While Facebook and Twitter are good for general contacts and possibly finding business, field-specific sites or sites that cater to professionals, like LinkedIn, are the best way to connect with people like you; however, don't stop at just posting your profile. Join groups on LinkedIn that fit your industry, alumni associations and former employers' groups. Look for people that you used to work with especially if they are still in the industry. Do searches for organizations and sites that are connected to your professional interests.

A blogs, short for web log, can be a way to connect with to connect with clients and others in your field. Blogs can be written in short frequent bursts or as longer, less frequent writings. When you are choosing a theme for your blog, focus on what your potential client might want to know. In my case it's writing advice. But remember, your blogs are another form of free advertising so make sure all of your contact information is available and, as always, remain professional.

Freelancing does take a certain amount of fearlessness and a willingness for shameless self-promotion--don't be shy. Get out into the real world too and attend conferences and events for your field of interest. Join professional organizations and read journals and note who is publishing and who is advertising. Pass out business cards to anyone who will take them, and

Sighted: The Freelancer's Union
The Freelancer's Union is a fantastic resource for any freelancers, and it provides an option for group insurance, job networking, events (both on and offline) and support. And best of all—membership is free. The Freelancer's Union is based out of New York, so all of the options aren't available to those not in the area, but the organization is becoming a powerful force and is a valuable tool for the telecommuting freelancer.
http://www.freelancersunion.org/

let the world know you are in business and ready to go.

Focusing on a Market

If you are a multi-talented person, it may be hard to narrow your scope to one market, but as a recruiter recently told me-this is the era of specialization. It's not enough to market yourself as a writer or even a technical writer, but you need to focus on a specific industry.

If you are a writer as I am, you have probably become a Jack or Jill of all trades, and you are better at some than others. There are dozens of specialties for writers, so focus on the few that appeal to you, you have direct experience with or you would like to learn more about. It goes without saying that this is true of most industries. Make yourself an expert in the field.

The same goes for other industries as well. It's not enough to be an accountant; you need to be a tax accountant, small business accountant or one of dozens of possibilities. If it is necessary, and it probably will be, take courses and get certifications in your areas of interest. Join professional groups, make contacts and ask a lot of questions.

Then focus on rewriting your resume to reflect the specialty and don't skimp. Have as many industry-specific resumes as you need, and consider tailoring resumes for each job you apply for. In addition, write a fresh cover letter to go along with the resume. It may seem like a lot of up-front work, but it will pay off in the end because you will be focusing your energy on relevant leads rather than taking a shotgun approach.

Chapter 3: Where the Jobs Are

If you're starting your telecommuting journey from scratch, your first step is to determine where to find jobs. Of course, this will partially depend on your career choice, but there are some basics. The Internet is littered with "Work-At-Home" offers, and you've probably gotten ads in your email. Careful! While there are plenty of genuine telecommuting jobs available, scams abound. Read the chapter on "Scams" before you even click on one of these advertisements.

There are legitimate websites dedicated to helping telecommuters find work, and the success is mixed. I've listed a few in the "Resources," but I can't make promises that you will find a job through these sites. Many of the sites simply repost what is already out there, and the jobs are often filled before they even reach the job site. Some of these are free to job-seekers and others charge a yearly fee, and while a fee is not necessarily a bad thing, do your homework to find out where the site gets its leads.

Sighted: SCORE

SCORE is a non-profit organization that pairs entrepreneurs with seasoned business people in their field. Most of the tools are free or low cost including mentoring, workshops and tools.

http://www.score.org/

Your first decision is whether or not you want a full or part time job with just one company or if you want to freelance or consult. This largely depends on your career choice, and there are pros and cons for both. It also depends on temperament, persistence and financial requirements. Weigh your needs and abilities carefully, and be honest with yourself.

The obvious perk of working for one company is security. In addition, you may have benefits like sick days, vacation and health insurance—all things you would need to factor into a freelancing budget. Steady work and a daily routine is a bonus too, but one of the unseen pluses is working with (albeit at a distance) with people you get to know. Sometimes working from home can be a lonely place, and human connections can raise spirits and productivity.

Security aside, there are downsides to working for a company. As a telecommuter, your possibility of advancement may be limited unless you want to work at least part time on site. The steadiness of a salary is nice, but you are confined to it too. Unless you have the option of working on commission, you aren't in charge of how much you can make.

Freelancing and/or consulting can give you a sense of empowerment. You decide which jobs you take, what you want to earn and the hours you work. If you want to give yourself a promotion, gear it up a notch and find better paying, more challenging jobs.

And freelancing can be terrifying for the same reasons. You are not only in charge of finding all of your work but getting paid too—sometimes that can be challenging. Health insurance, often a huge expense, needs to be factored into your budget and so does time off. You'll soon find out that vacations are necessary sanity savers when you work from a home office, and nobody is paying you if you aren't working.

Having worked both for a company and as a freelancer, I prefer freelancing—most of the time. I love the challenge of a new project and meeting new people. I like being in charge of what I make, and I have a more flexible schedule. What I don't like is the inevitable slow times and the huge health insurance bill every month. There have been times that I have worked through the night to get a project finished, and I often start work at 6:00 a.m. And I am sometimes simply weary of continuously having to sell myself.

If freelancing feels right to you, then do an frank evaluation. If you have a spouse with a back-up income and health insurance, that is a big plus. If not, save enough money for a few months of little to no work especially in the beginning. You can always start with a company job and move to freelancing if you need to get your bearings telecommuting before you jump into freelancing.

Online Job Sites

The Internet is filled with job sites—some good, some bad, and some very ugly scams. I'm resisting making too many recommendations in this book because the sites change so often, and what may be great one day may not be so effectual after a buy-out or management change. With that being said, the Internet remains a viable place to find jobs.

While it certainly doesn't hurt to put your resume and job information on one of the big online job sites, and anytime you can get your information out there for free it's worth doing, keep a few things in mind. These sites work to the advantage of the employer who pays a fee to find just the right employee, and this could literally be out of tens of thousands. It doesn't mean you won't get the job; it just means that the competition is fierce. Having been on the hiring side of some of the big sites, I can tell you that often the choices are so overwhelming that there is no other option than to blindly choose at times. Some of the employers trolling these sites are scammers too. The sites certainly don't promote scams, and do what they can to stop them, but they are simply too big to be aware of the actions of all of the employers. There is a lot of irrelevance too. Even though there is nothing in my resume that suggests that I might be open to insurance sales, I get a large amount of these email offers that I can track back to the mega-job sites.

There are other sites that specialize in finding candidates telecommuting jobs, and they're a mixed bag. While this does focus your search better, it is no guarantee of getting viable jobs. It doesn't take long on these sites to see that a portion of the "jobs" listed are either non-paying or very low paying. Many of these posts are outsourced overseas, and it is tough to make any real money from them. Some have shady reputations too. I had a spooky encounter from a person who said he had a job for me, but I would have to provide him with my bank account information so I could get paid. I couldn't get away from that site fast enough.

Other telecommuting sites are legit, and some will charge for the full listing. This is not necessarily a bad thing, but do some research into the company before you part with your cash. Run searches on the name of the company and key words like "review," "scam" and "effective." Be objective about the results and do some serious critical thinking about what you find.

The best way to find jobs online, however, is metaphorically hitting the pavement and going old school. Sit down with pen and paper, or keyboard, and make a list of places you would like to work, and remember—you aren't limited to those in your town. Then start scouring their websites one at a time. Get a feel for the company's values to see if it is a good fit for you by reading press releases and the corporate philosophy statements. Do searches to see what employees think about working for the company, and join the LinkedIn group if possible. Usually at the bottom of the company's home page, you'll see a hyperlink for jobs, and most companies will either list openings or have a contact form or email address to write for more information. Remember though, if the listings are for on-site jobs, you'll have a difficult time convincing a company that you cold called that you can do the same job from home if you don't have a history with them.

The most effective way of finding a telecommuting job online is the same as finding an offline job: network. Find like-minded people in your field and pick their brains; attend conventions and conferences and spread the business cards around, and use any current contacts you may have.

Scams

Predators lure people in because they appeal to a basic need, and work is certainly no exception. When the economy is bad, they smell blood and will stop at nothing to suck you into a scam. I'm not trying to scare you, but I am trying to make you more aware.

Any, and I repeat ANY, job that you have to make a payment to work should be avoided. Any offer that claims you will make a ton of money fast with little or no work is a scam. And any job that requires you to sign up more people to do the same job to make money is multi-level marketing—beware.

Some of the most notorious scams have been around for years and made the crossover from ads in the back of magazines to the Internet:

- Assembly work
- Stuffing envelopes
- Medical billing and typing that requires you to pay for your work
- Chain letters

And there are a few new twists:

- Spamming
- Calling 900 numbers for information (there's a hefty charge)
- Social networking posters

Sighted: The Better Business Bureau Work at home schemes: http://www.bbb.org/us/article/work-at-home-schemes-408

In addition to the outright scams, you'll find quite a few jobs that are legitimate but nearly impossible to make much money at. Most writers are familiar with content writing jobs. I've taken some myself to gain experience and fill in the lean times, and there are a few that pay a reasonable amount of money if you are fast, but most pay pennies for a 300 word article. Some of the multi-level marketing companies have been around for decades and work within the confines of the law, but due to the nature of the business, you probably aren't going to make much, if anything. There are a number of companies that will pay for you to fill out forms or surveys, and while you can make money, it's not enough to live on.

Unscrupulous companies and individuals with also attempt to steal your identity so keep your personal information to yourself unless you have researched a company thoroughly. Above all, do not give out your social security number or banking information unless you have been hired and you are sure it is a legitimate business. Ultimately you will have to release your personal data for tax and legal reasons, but if red flags go up, walk away and find another job.

The best way to avoid being scammed is to become an informed consumer of information. Do your research, and don't skimp. Look for reviews on the company, check to see if they are listed with the Better Business Bureau or their local chamber of commerce and connect with former and current employees.

Scammers can be extremely clever. While researching for this book, I ran across a site that appeared to be a consumer advocate warning about job scams. When I clicked on a link that invited me to learn more about scams, it took me to the real purpose of the site: a get rich quick scheme.

I was also offered a job via email with a company supposedly was from Finland. The email was in extremely broken English, and promised me $2,000 a month for 10 to 15 hours a week work accepting and reshipping packages. My savvy husband, Detective William Trobaugh, Ret., spotted this as a familiar scam right away. Not only would I have been participating in an illegal activity, my first and last paycheck would be counterfeit.

If you are taken in by scammers, you do have resources but don't expect to get back any lost money. Any type of fraud involving the USPS needs to be reported at https://postalinspectors.uspis.gov/forms/MailFraud Complaint.aspx. If you have been given a money order for payment, you can verify whether it is counterfeit or not by calling 1-866-459-7822.

Reporting Internet scams is a little trickier. First make sure you protect yourself. If you gave out any personal information like a Social Security number or credit card or bank account numbers, notify credit reporting agencies, your bank and credit card companies. Order your credit reports from all three agencies and monitor them for discrepancies. Report the incident to your local law enforcement agency and get the report. Don't expect them to be able to do anything, but it's important to leave a paper trail. Local law enforcement's hands are tied by jurisdiction restrictions, but they should be notified nonetheless. If your identity has been stolen, report it to the Federal Trade Commission: http://www.ftc.gov/bcp/edu/microsites/idtheft/consumers/defend.html. A complete list of identity

> **Sighted: Reshipping Scams**
> *If you're offered a job to accept merchandise in your home and reship it for a company, please read this notice from the US Postal Service and do not take the job no matter how tempting it sounds.*
>
> *https://postalinspectors.uspis.gov/radDocs/consumer/ReshippingScam.html#AcceptJob*

theft guidelines can be found on the Privacy Rights Clearinghouse website: http://www.privacyrights.org/fs/fs17a.htm.

The bottom line is that no matter how desperate you are or how good the deal sounds, research the company, think critically and if it sounds too good to be true, it is.

Best Bets

While the multitude of scams is the bad news, the good news is that there are plenty of legitimate opportunities to telecommute. While online sources are always an option to find jobs, consider going low-tech. Start connecting with former co-workers and employers. If you left on good terms, ask for letters of recommendation or references. Let people know that you are interested in telework and that you have put thought and effort into the planning.

If you are presently working, don't forget that there may be opportunities within your company that you don't know about, or you can create your own.

They know you and trust you so do your homework
and develop a convincing case.

Chapter 4: Office Space

When it comes to setting up a home office, you have a lot of latitude. While there are some necessities to all telecommuters' offices, much depends on the industry, money, space and personal needs. If you are working for a company, check with your supervisor to see what you will need and what the company will provide. As you are setting up your office, don't forget to keep receipts for everything that you buy. Not only is it the best way not to get carried away buying goodies, but it's also tax deductable.

The Basics

Brick and Mortar

The size and complexity of your office will usually depend on your available space. While it is possible to do your work at your kitchen table, you'll find you are more productive when you have a dedicated work space set up with the items you need close at hand. Take a creative look around your home. If you are lucky enough to have an office or spare bedroom then you need go no further. But if space is short, get creative. Take the doors off of a closet and turn it into a mini-office; clean out a corner of the basement or garage or find a nook or corner you can call your own.

Furniture

There are two essentials for your office that can't be underestimated: a desk and a good chair. Before you buy or make a desk, think about your needs as a worker. The size will somewhat be dictated by your office space, but be realistic about what your need your desk to do. It should be big enough for your computer with some space left over. But there may be other items you need to keep close at hand:

- Phone
- Lighting
- Office supplies
- Books or manuals
- Papers
- Printer

If you are short on space, think about basics. If you don't need the phone all the time, just keep a cordless or cell phone nearby. You can use overhead lights or a floor lamp instead of a desk lamp and a folding table can hold papers and books when you need them and they can be stored when you don't. When I need extra desk space for a project, I put up a TV tray to hold the papers I need nearby.

Even if you're on a tight budget, spending a little extra on a good office chair is worth it. With luck, you will be spending a good deal of time sitting in it, and you'll be more productive longer in a good chair. An office chair should swivel and have adjustable heights, have a back with lumbar support, a width of at least 18 inches and be made of a comfortable material. While prices vary wildly and gimmicks abound, you can find a suitable chair for under $100. If you have the cash to spare, there are all sorts of ergonomic designs with high-tech materials that may or may not be worth it.

You may also need storage depending on what you are working on, and this can include a bookcase, filing cabinet, storage bins and accordion files. If you are short on space, stores like Ikea and Crate and Barrel specialize in compact and functional designs, but don't ignore the low to no cost favorites like plastic milk carriers. A trip to a thrift shop can also yield some low-cost storage finds as well. Take your time and plan your space for both comfort and productivity.

Technology

The backbone of the telecommuter's office is a computer. Chances are you already own one or two along with various other electronic devices. However, you may have to update or modify to make your computer work for your telecommuting. It took me a few attempts to discover what worked for me: a 14" laptop that works well for travel and that I could connect it to a large monitor at home. Analyze your own needs—will you be traveling or going to an office part time, do you need a lot of storage, will you need special software? Ask people in your field what works for them, and discuss options with a technician so you know the selections in your price range. In addition to a computer, there are few other necessities:

- High speed Internet—dial-up won't do it, and most companies will require it.
- Good virus and malware protection program—people won't want to hire you if you send them viruses.
- A way to back up data—either an external hard drive or off-site storage. Not only should you have it, you should use it on a regular basis.
- Dedicated phone—a cell phone or an extra line. At the very least have caller-ID, and answer the phone with your company's name if you don't recognize the number. It pays to check out some of the VIOP options too.
- Printer/scanner—at some time you will have to deal with paper or make a copy.

You may also find that you need a few extras:

- Fax machine—this can be combined with the printer; although, I've found this a little awkward.
- Phone headset—this is a must for comfort if you are on the phone a lot.
- Shredder—if you do work with physical documents, the safest way to dispose of them is to shred them.

And then there are the goodies:

- Tablet—great for travel.
- Smart-phone—if you are on the run, this can keep you connected and save space.
- Business document copier—this is a small device that can copy and organize business cards, documents and receipts.

Office Supplies

These are the little things that you don't think about until they aren't there. Start with the basics and you can add to your collections as the need arises. It's easy to get carried away when shopping in an office supply big box store, so take a list to keep it reasonable.

- Pens and pencils—don't forget a pencil sharpener and a holder.
- Hole punch
- Note pad—yes, you will still need to take notes by hand at times.
- Scissors
- Tape
- Sticky notes
- Highlighters

- Files
- Stapler and staples
- Envelopes
- Stamps
- Calendar—whether it is virtual or physical, don't trust your memory for important deadlines and appointments.

Perhaps the most important office supply is a good-quality business card. While you can print your own on a printer, there are some great deals online that may even be less expensive. Take your time with the design and do a careful proofreading before you order though.

Chapter 5: The Case Against Telecommuting

It's no secret that some managers and workplaces are not exactly lavishing praise for telework. While some cite legitimate concerns, other issues can be overcome with creativity and facts. The list for reasons not to allow employees to telecommute is long: legalities, lack of oversight, company policies and security to name a few. Let's face it; there are some gray areas that need to be addressed and overcome before telecommuting is widely accepted.

Legalities

A serious and legitimate concern employers have with telecommuting is the application of federal and state laws. Employment attorneys are cautious as well; the area is too new and diverse for concrete standards. And this potential liability extends to all telecommuters whether it is an occasional Friday working from home or full time. All of this makes potential employers nervous and wondering why they should go to the trouble.

Some of the concerns are easy to overcome. Taxes are an issue, but there are already provisions in place for traditional workers who live in a state other than the one they work in. If your employer deducts the state tax, you may have to file a separate non-resident return; however, you may have taxes from both states withheld depending on the state tax laws. But don't panic; when it comes time to file you'll be refunded the amount from your employer's state. Your employer's human resource department will walk you through the tax issues, but if you are confused don't hesitate to contact a professional tax expert.

If you are a consultant or freelancer and work for several companies either on a regular or one-time basis, taxes can get pretty complicated. At times, I have worked as an hourly employee on a regular basis, as a consultant or I've been paid per article I've written or royalties over a period of time. I don't think my situation is unusual. If you are sharp with taxes, you can do your own, but they give me a headache, so I hire an accountant. I've found the cost isn't much more than having taxes done by a national company, and I have a year-to-year relationship with my accountant. Just make sure you save all of your receipts and pay information, and keep things reasonably organized.

OSHA and other federal and state employee laws come into play as well. Since most of us sit at a chair in front of a computer while we are teleworking, it doesn't seem to be an issue, but all scenarios need to be taken into consideration especially from an employer's point of view. State Employee Compensation and the Americans with Disabilities Act also pose problems. Filing a claim, if you are hurt while teleworking, is problematic because of the lack of witnesses and unusual circumstances. Most employers will insist that you file an injury report just as you would if you were on-site. Disabled telecommuters can expect the same reasonable accommodations in a home office as they do in an on-site workplace, and it shouldn't be a problem. But when home and office space is blurred, it can get overwhelming for both sides.

The Fair Labor Standards Act insures employees are fairly paid for the hours worked, but logging a telecommuter's hours isn't always cut and dried. Many telecommuting professions have exempt status, but it is a very gray area. Additionally, some states have mandatory break laws, and this is virtually impossible to enforce in a home office situation. Some employers will ask you to sign a form saying that you promise to take the required breaks, but for some it is a non-issue. In addition, the laws in the state where the physical business is located may be different than in the state where you telework.

Of great concern to employers is security. With more businesses becoming part of the global marketplace, the competition is fiercer for fewer markets, and loss of trade secrets, proprietary information and data are realistic issues. When computers and personnel are on-site, it's easier to keep tabs on proprietary information and people, but off-site is a little more difficult to control. The obvious answer is to incorporate contracts and work with the most trustworthy of employees, but in some cases, more precautions are needed. The problem of the mobile office has been around for a while—sales people and executives have been traveling with laptops for some time. Companies often apply the same standards to a telecommuter and provide hardware, software and support for teleworkers.

An even greater security risk is working on government contracts. While the bulk of federal contracts don't require security clearance, those that do are treated quite differently. Because of the Telework Act of 2010, this issue has become more common, and contractors also have to deal with security clearance and off-site work. Most of the time the problem is solved by teleworkers doing the security work from a secure telework center; however, these are only available in the Washington, DC area. Other provisions can be made, but expect any work with a security clearance requirement to be handled differently than the average telecommute job.iv

Sighted: Reasonable Accommodation
Disabled teleworkers have the same legal rights that they do in the physical workplace. Read more about your rights at The U.S. Equal Employment Opportunity Commission's website.

http://www.eeoc.gov/facts/telework.html

Other issues that come up as well, including sick days, discrimination and dismissal, all take some adjustments for the telecommuter, but most companies have working policies that will cover the situations. I've found that most organizations are very cooperative, and the accommodations usually aren't too great. Once when doing work for a federal contractor, I had to take a drug test. It took a few phone calls and the aid of UPS, but the HR manager and I managed to work it out.

While most of these issues can be handled by the company's HR department, zoning compliance is on the shoulders of the telecommuter. These laws vary widely depending on your region, and some areas have no zoning laws at all. Before making a commitment to telecommute, make sure you know your local laws and that you comply. What seems like a non-issue now, can become a very big legal headache in the future.

While all of this may seem discouraging, keep in mind that most of these regulations are things that human resource departments deal with on a daily basis—only the location has changed. If your company cites these as roadblocks in your telecommuting highway, remind them that there are fairly simple solutions to any of these issues.

The Unmanageable Manager

I once worked for a manager who appeared both resentful and confused by telecommuting. She was a genuinely nice person but was also clearly uninformed about telework. I never seemed to clearly understand her goals or instructions, and she got annoyed if I called and emailed a lot. I was frustrated because I didn't have enough information to complete the job efficiently, and I felt I had to guess at the expectations.

Managers may see telecommuting as an extra workload for them and have concerns about time management; after all, it's tough enough to keep people you can see motivated and going in the right direction. Most experienced telecommuters have stories about nightmare bosses and those who felt at ease with the situation, and they can tell you what makes the difference.

I hesitate to call them "bad" managers; they may be very effective with on-site employees, but these are supervisors who don't handle the telecommuting situation very well. They may be resentful about what seems to them as extra work on their part, the inability to visually monitor an employee or a general mistrust of the policy and conditions. They may make your life miserable by over or even under communicating with you. You may find it difficult to understand exactly what he or she expects of you and become frustrated. Obviously, bad management boils down to low productivity, and the manager may blame this on the teleworker rather than her or himself.

Granted, the bad boss dilemma isn't solely a telecommuting problem, but it does crop up on occasion. It's not the end of the world or even your telework career, but it can make your like very difficult and hurt your professional reputation. There are two ways you can go about solving the problem—educate and adapt.

The education solution may make you a little squeamish if you don't know your supervisor very well. The trick is to do it in a way that that doesn't threaten your manager—try the honest approach. Simply say that you know the situation is new for everybody and that you welcome any guidance or information. Offer any information that your find helpful—there is a list of links in the resource section that might be helpful in your quest to educate.

As leaders, mangers have the responsibility to make sure that you have the information and materials to complete the job adequately. But because more than 50 percent of communication is visual, managers need to compensate. In a PowerPoint presentation for mangers, SHRM, the Society for Human Resource Management, underscores the importance of adapting communications skills for telecommuters.

- Make sure all goals and deadlines are clearly communicated.
- Confer with IT to make sure all technological options are available for adequate communication and work.
- Develop a methodology for monitoring and assigning tasks.
- If possible, arrange for occasional face-to-face communication.
- Encourage open communication and trust.

Sighted: A Guide to Telework in the Federal Government This guide has some handy tips for teleworkers and managers in general.

I've put a link to the entire PowerPoint in the resource section.

In addition, managers should be responsible for knowing the company's telecommuting policy and laws that may affect it. In order to overcome the telecommuting problem of isolation, set regularly scheduled times to talk about any issues, and don't forget to keep the teleworker informed about changes or updates in the project. Yes, it is more work, but it is also a manager's job to create effective communication pathways and foster a relationship with his or her team.

However, the burden of successful communication isn't solely the responsibility of the manager. Telecommuters should become informed about policies and laws as well and communicate needs clearly. If you work for multiple companies, you become adept at reading the comfort levels of managers. It becomes easier to lead conversations and emails in directions that clarify the goals and expectations. One trick I use is to always rephrase what is said to me. For example, I might say, "Let me see if I understand. You would like the proposals edited and proofread in AP style by 4:00 Wednesday." In that short sentence I've clarified the details and the time-frame.

Chapter 6: Motivation

The biggest argument that resistant managers have against telework is that they are not able to motivate their staff. If most of communication is non-verbal, then how can a manager effectively motivate? Conversely, telecommuters complain about not being able to motivate themselves. I admit that there are days that I'm simply running low on inspiration. While the solitude can be refreshing, isolation is stifling.

It's easy for management and staff to point motivational fingers at each other, but the truth is that motivation has to be an equal responsibility. Managers have the obligation to educate themselves to inspire teleworkers—it's a different medium but not an impossible task. But telecommuters have a responsibility too. Workers need to develop a system to keep their interest and production high. Let's face it, whether or not you think it's fair, telecommuters usually have to prove themselves as responsible and time-conscious workers to justify working from home.

Do a search for the key words 'motivation' and 'work' and you'll get thousands of suggestions, posters, articles and ads for consultants. There are psychological and sociological studies and a multitude of theories and models. Government studies have been done, and universities publish extensively on the subject. And if on-site motivation is a problem, how can telecommuters and their managers cope?

The Creative Manager

Despite some fears, teleworkers are usually more focused and productive than traditional workers. Reasons vary, but one study cites the savings in commute time, the relaxed atmosphere and lack of interruptions as reasons telecommuters seem to produce more.v However, the same study found that both employees and managers have to work harder to develop a good relationship. There are tactics that managers can employ to increase the motivation of their telecommuting staff:

- Try new things, and if it doesn't work, move onto another idea.
- If possible, schedule face-to-face meetings.

- Recognize achievements and accomplishments either through official channels or through praise—preferably both.
- Remember birthdays and professional milestones. Cake in the break room may not work, but a card or small gift makes anyone feel appreciated.

The on-site culture can't be entirely replicated for the teleworker, but regular communications with clear goals along with recognition of accomplishments will go a long way to motivate the telecommuter.

Self-Motivation

If you're old enough, you may remember Saturday Night Live's Stuart Smalley-Al Franken's co-dependent character with a low self esteem issue. His overly-sugary mantra was, "I'm good enough; I'm smart enough, and, doggone it, people like me!" That might be a slightly overboard, but a little self-affirmation isn't a bad thing.

While most of us enjoy the solitude of telecommuting and feel that we are more productive in an off-site environment, there are times when isolation from co-workers can be counterproductive. We do and should look to our bosses for motivation, but we have to be proactive and create our own incentives too.

Most experts agree that setting goals is the first step. That in itself can help you get over the motivational hurdle. But as we all know from failed New Year's resolutions that setting a goal is only the first step. Although getting paid is a powerful factor, creating personal goals and rewards are very effective. Devise your own set of rewards that will work for you and dole them out as you hit your mile markers:

- Break a project down into manageable sections. Looking at the big picture might be overwhelming.
- Set up break times to clear your mind when you complete a task—go for a walk, exercise or do whatever works for you.
- Long-term goals deserve larger rewards. Depending on what is reasonable for your situation consider taking a vacation, go shopping, visiting friends or reading a book.

- Keep your rewards positive. Don't feed a bad habit (smoking, drinking, over eating etc.) as a reward for completing a task.
- Analyze what is getting in your way. I hit a wall when writing this book. When I evaluated why I was frustrated, I realized that the scope of the project had shifted slightly and some chapters weren't fitting. When I scrapped them and substituted others, then I was able to work past the roadblocks.
- Avoid striving for perfection. Although that may sound self-defeating, just the thought of a project being perfect can freeze the best of us. Accept your flaws and work toward the very best you can achieve.

Remember that motivation is a self-fulfilling prophesy. The more success you have, the more motivated you are.

Chapter 7: When to Call It Quits

It's difficult to move away from a commitment, but sometimes situations call for it. If you find that, for whatever reason, telecommuting is not for you, then you shouldn't look at it as a failure but as another steppingstone in your professional development.

Research is limited, but a study from UC Davis suggests that nearly half of all telecommuters leave after 30 months vi. Reasons range from changes within company structure to simply not being compatible with working from home. Depending on whether teleworkers work for one company or freelance, are part-time or full, has an impact on decisions to stay or leave.

Reasons for leaving telecommuting vary:

- Left company
- Change in structure
- Promotion
- Downsizing
- Not making enough money

- Lack of benefits
- Telecommuting doesn't fit personality
- Telecommuting doesn't fit job description
- Too many distractions
- Change in home situation

At times, the decision to leave telecommuting may not be the worker's choice as with changes within the company. A change in supervisor may also be a determining factor—some bosses simply don't understand or like the dynamics of telework. And there are times too that supervisors feel that the telecommuter's performance and output is not satisfactory.

Freelancers and consultants are particularly vulnerable. The very nature of the business has its ups and downs, and sometimes freelancers simply get weary of the constant job hunt. Financial burdens like paying for insurance out-of-pocket and meeting responsibilities during low-work times can be overwhelming as well.

Whatever the reason, the telecommuting experience shouldn't be viewed as a waste of time. If you have discovered it simply isn't for you, you have at least gained that insight and probably have sharpened your productivity skills. If you've left for financial reasons, you can always return to telecommuting when your personal or professional situation changes.

Chapter 8: Advice from the Pros

No one can give better advice than the people in the trenches—the telecommuting professional. Most telecommuters would tell you that there are ups and downs to telework, and most wouldn't give it up for a traditional workplace.

Esther Driggs works as a marketing representative for an international company along with several dozen others on the team. She says she wouldn't go back to a traditional work setting, but there are both positives and negatives:

"I think that for some reason when involved in conference calls with coworkers, there is a complete
lack of respect among some workers. Yes there are learning curves, but I am sure that if everyone were sitting in a conference room, there would not be the lack of professionalism that there is on the phone. Perhaps it is because people are in their comfort zones."

She also says that friends and family sometimes think that because she is at home her time is freer. "They don't seem to understand that you still have to dedicate a set amount of hours each day for work."

On the flip-side, telecommuting ultimately allows her more time for her family, "The thing that I enjoy the most about telecommuting is the flexibility. I do not have to miss out on any activities with my kids or try to come up with day care when they are sick of out of school."

Win Rayburn, who is not only a seasoned telecommuter but also my father, says that without technology, telecommuting in his field of engineering wouldn't be possible, "After I retired, I started doing design work at home and without the Internet or computers this would have been impossible in the past. I was able to communicate with customers, send designs, quotes and invoices electronically all from home." Working for a company located not far from his house, he was also able to "make occasional stops to the plant more as "good will". "

As a freelance writer and editor, Lisa Godfrey sees the biggest hurdle in working from home is not finding motivation but being able to stop working to give herself time to recharge. She says, "For extended periods of time, I've worked way too many hours because the work is always "calling" to me. While others were enjoying their weekends, I'd be at the computer working. My challenge is toning down my drive to complete a project or not get a jump on something I know may be coming up next week."

Lisa also has a lot to say about the telephone in a home office:

"1. If you're self-employed, allocate the funds to pay for home office telephone service that is distinctly separate from all other personal telephones. If you're an off-site staff worker, ask your
employer to pay for this service.

2. Use your home office telephone number exclusively for your telecommuting work. Resist the impulse
to give the number to friends and family.

3. Do everything you can to keep your home office telephone ringer from sounding in your personal living space. Unplug or turn off the phone when

you're off-hours if necessary. When you're "home," you
need the separation from work, and if you can hear your office telephone ringing from your bedroom, you can say goodbye to relaxation. Just remember to turn it back on or plug it in when you're back on the clock, because no one will believe you "forgot" something that important."

Co-author of *7 Days to Forget* and author of *7 Lives Remembered*, Gayle Brown, argues that interruptions, although maddening, can be useful, "The space you work in is not respected like an office outside the home, nor do most people think you are really working when you are home. Interruptions are also much more frequent. As a writer, I find that no matter how irritating the interruptions are they are also what occupies my writer's mind and guides the thought processes toward solid personal reflection through the shear focus required to stay on task or return to task. It becomes a matter of multi-listening and multi-refocusing, rather than mindlessly multi-tasking in an office environment. This process brings a much broader and more personal aspect to writing. Embrace the interruptions. Some of the best ideas come through them."

Gayle is also quick to point out that, "Working from home has plenty of perks. Having morning coffee in pajamas, taking the laptop outside on a pretty day, being able to record that flash of an idea when it hits and having control over your environment are just a few."

Matt Savage, a manager at an Ohio technical company, represents the other side of the equation: a supervisor of a telecommuter. Matt states that over communication is key for a successful relationship between a company and a telecommuting employee. "The commuter should understand
the needs and expectations of the business. Once these are understood, communicate to see if the "relationship" is working. If it is not working as the business or telecommuter envisioned this needs to be discovered and adjusted early in the process."

Chapter 9: Happily Ever After

Some of my most rewarding and most terrifying professional moments have been telecommuting. I would find it hard to give up the flexibility and potential. Frankly, there's even an element of excitement—who knows what incredible opportunity will crop up tomorrow? I've gotten to travel to exciting places; I've met interesting people, and unlike a traditional job, my income can increase greatly in a short period of time.

And that is also why I find it terrifying. There have been long dry periods, and other times the only pay offered was far below what I was worth. I am responsible for my technology, my expenses, my insurance and my next job. Taxes are a nightmare, and sometimes I have to work around the clock to get all of my assignments finished.

 Of course those of you who work for a single company don't have the same problems, but there are others: isolation, people who don't think you are working, distractions and lack of support to name just a few. There is a rising sentiment that telecommuting damages career advancement, and many employees feel forgotten and left out of the corporate communication loop.

But despite the disadvantages, telecommuting is growing, and more individuals and companies are considering it as a viable option. For those of us who have chosen telework as a long-term lifestyle, it's hard to imagine working any other way. We thrive on the independence and potential of telework, and we work through the difficulties.

> **Sighted: Happiness and Telecommuting Studies**
> Science Daily's article on the psychological benefits of telecommuting captures the data from several studies.
>
> http://www.sciencedaily.com/releases/2007/11/071119182930.htm

If you are new to telecommuting, you may be feeling some of the frustrations more acutely. In my early days, I felt like I was in an unknown territory. Every disappointment felt like a major disaster, and even my successes were met with suspicion. As time passed, I became more adept at dealing with the issues, and my problem-solving ability increased tremendously. My situation is far from unique; many veteran telecommuters will tell you that there is an adjustment period.

For those of you considering telecommuting, but haven't taken the plunge, I urge you to do your homework. Not only should you take a hard look at your industry but yourself as well. Do you have the personality for independent work? Studies show that extroverted, self-disciplined people make the most successful telecommuters, but I've met people who are quiet and feel comfortable working amidst clutter and are doing very well at telework.

Whether you are an old pro or an eager newbie, it's hard to deny that telework is an exciting ride. It forces you to become insightful and resourceful and tests your skills and abilities. It will lead you through new avenues of your career and personal life. Telecommuting can give you an exhilarating sense of freedom and command of your own future as well as the flexibility to enhance your family and personal life.

Welcome to the journey, fellow telecommuter.

About the Author

Catherine Rayburn-Trobaugh is the owner of CRT Commercial Writing and Word Branch Publishing. She has a Bachelor's degree in English from Wilmington College of Ohio and a Master's degree in writing and literature from Wright State University. Catherine has taught college-level writing and literature since 1992 and has been a professional writer for more than 25 years.

Her love of hiking and outdoor activities brought her, her husband Bill, and their two dogs—Asher and Ozzie—to the mountains of Western North Carolina where they live in a log cabin at the edge of the Nantahala National Forest.

Contact

I would love to hear from you. If you have a telecommuting experience that you would like to share or you have a question, please email me at catherine@wordbranch.com. Don't forget to sign up for my blogs: http://wordbranch.com/the-field-guide-to-telecommuting-resource-page.html

If you are a writer interested in e-publishing your book, Word Branch Publishing would like to talk to you: http://wordbranch.com.

If you liked The Field Guide to Telecommuting, please leave feedback.
http://www.amazon.com/The-Field-Guide-Telecommuting-ebook/dp/B007XF35HK/ref=sr_1_6?ie=UTF8&qid=1335721587&sr=8-6

Resources

I try to find the most relevant websites for the resource page, but I can't personally vouch for these. Websites change and disappear, so be wise when using the information. I will keep an updated resource page at http://wordbranch.com/the-field-guide-to-telecommuting-resource-page.html for access for the purchasers of this e-book.

Career Assessment Tools:

Monster: http://my.monster.com/Career-Management/Landing.aspx?WT.srch=1&WT.mc_n=olm11gsrchcar

Career Intelligence: http://www.career-intelligence.com/assessment/career_assessment.asp

Career Explorer:
http://www.careerexplorer.net/aptitude.asp

Helpful Information:

Online juror: https://onlineverdict.com/jurors.php

The Telework Coalition: http://www.telcoa.org/

SHRM PowerPoint for Managers:
http://www.google.com/url?sa=t&rct=j&q=&esrc=s
&source=web&cd=1&ved=0CCMQFjAA&url=http%3
A%2F%2Fwww.shrm.org%2FTemplatesTools%2FSa
mples%2FPowerPoints%2FDocuments%2F09-PPT-
Making%2520Telecommuting%2520Work.pptx&ei=
R959T_28OoaC8QS3ltDtDA&usg=AFQjCNHa32XulTY
Y4xz-
NMqNSCiQiBDIGw&sig2=FW0P_B6AO4IIFrfTBZ_kzg

Call to verify a money order: 1-866-459-7822.

USPS report mail fraud:
https://postalinspectors.uspis.gov/forms/MailFraud
Complaint.aspx

Federal Trade Commission Identity Theft:
http://www.ftc.gov/bcp/edu/microsites/idtheft/co
nsumers/defend.html

Privacy Rights Clearinghouse:
http://www.privacyrights.org/fs/fs17a.htm

The American Telecommuting Association
http://www.yourata.com/telecommuting/

Statistics for telecommuting
http://www.teleworkresearchnetwork.com/pros-cons

Government security suggestions:
http://www.itl.nist.gov/lab/bulletns/archives/telecomm.htm

References

Department of Labor Career Assessment Tools:
http://www.doleta.gov/jobseekers/assess_yourself.cfm

O*Net: http://www.onetcenter.org/

Status of Telework in the Federal Government:
http://www.telework.gov/Reports_and_Studies/Annual_Reports/2010teleworkreport.pdf

Telework Research Network:
http://www.teleworkresearchnetwork.com/telecommuting-statistics

Telework Research Network -The Latest Telecommuting Statistics:

http://www.teleworkresearchnetwork.com/telecommuting-statistics

Transportation Implications of Telecommuting:
http://ntl.bts.gov/DOCS/telecommute.html

UC Davis Telecommuting Study:
http://www.its.ucdavis.edu/tcenters/repts/interim/Ch5.htm

World at Work Organization: Special Report:
http://www.worldatwork.org/waw/adimLink?id=53034

End Notes

[i] The State of California Telework – Telecommuting Program
1983 – 21St Century
http://www.documents.dgs.ca.gov/dgs/pio/telework/1983-21st%20Century%20Program.pdf

[ii] Data from Telework 2011 A WorldatWork Special Report

[iii] Statistics from the Telework Research Network:
http://www.teleworkresearchnetwork.com/pros-cons

[iv] Security Clearance Survey
http://www.clearancejobs.com/files/CompensationSurvey2012.pdf

[v] U.S. Office of Personnel Management: TELEWORK WORKS: A Compendium of Success Stories
http://www.opm.gov/studies/FINAL-TELEWRK.htm#Methodology

[vi] Data derived from a University of California at Davis study on telecommuting.

Catherine Rayburn-Trobaugh